MAIN

Chemicals
in Action

Materials
Changes &
Reactions

Chris Oxlade

Heinemann Library
Chicago, Illinois

© 2002 Reed Educational & Professional Publishing
Published by Heinemann Library,
an imprint of Reed Educational & Professional Publishing,
Chicago, Illinois

Customer Service 888-454-2279

Visit our website at www.heinemannlibrary.com

Designed by Tinstar Design
Illustrations by Jeff Edwards
Originated by Ambassador Litho
Printed by Wing King Tong in Hong Kong

06 05 04 03
10 9 8 7 6 5 4 3 2

Library of Congress Cataloging-in-Publication Data
Oxlade, Chris.
  Materials changes and reactions / Chris Oxlade.
      p. cm. -- (Chemicals in action)
Includes bibliographical references and index.
  ISBN 1-58810-197-5
  1. Chemical reactions--Juvenile literature. 2. Strength of materials--Juvenile literature. [1. Chemical reactions.] I. Title.
  QD501 .O92 2001
  541.3'9--dc21

                              2001000105

Acknowledgments
The Publishers would like to thank the following for permission to reproduce photographs: pp. 18, 21, 28, 36 Andrew Lambert; p. 13 Bruce Coleman; p. 32 Chris Honeywell; pp. 26, 34 Environmental Images; p. 19 Faltner; p. 8 Food Features; p. 31 Hulton Getty; pp. 17, 28 (bottom) Peter Gould; p. 38 Robert Harding; p. 5 Russell Hobbs; pp. 4, 11, 12, 14, 23, 24, 27, 29, 31 Science Photo Library; p. 7 Shout; pp. 9, 15, 25, 33, 35, 37 Trevor Clifford; p. 6 Tudor photography.

Cover photograph reproduced with permission of Image Bank.

The publishers would like to thank Ted Dolter and Dr. Nigel Saunders for their assistance in the preparation of this book.

Some words are shown in bold, **like this.** You can find out what they mean by looking in the glossary.

Contents

Chemicals in Action

What's the connection among a violent explosion, a kettle that changes color when it boils, and the leaves of a plant? The answer is material changes and reactions. They are all examples of substances changing to produce new substances. Our knowledge of how materials change and react with each other is used in making chemicals, medical research, and engineering.

The study of material changes and reactions is part of the science of chemistry. Many people think of chemistry as something that scientists study by doing experiments in laboratories with special equipment. This part of chemistry is very important. It is how scientists figure out what substances are made of and how they make new materials—but this is only a tiny part of chemistry. Most chemistry occurs away from laboratories, in factories and chemical plants. Chemistry is used to manufacture an enormous range of items, such as synthetic fibers for fabrics, drugs to treat diseases, explosives for fireworks, **solvents** for paints, and fertilizers for crops.

*When the chemicals glycerol and potassium permanganate are mixed, the **chemical change** that occurs creates a lot of heat.*

About the experiments

There are several experiments in this book for you to try. They will help you to understand some of the chemistry in the book. An experiment is designed to help solve a scientific problem. Scientists use a logical approach to experiments so that they can conclude things from the results. A scientist first writes down a hypothesis, which he or she thinks might be the answer to the problem, then designs an experiment to test the hypothesis. He or she then writes down the results of the experiment and concludes whether or not the results show the hypothesis to be correct. We only know what we do about chemistry because scientists have carefully carried out millions of experiments over hundreds of years. Experiments have allowed scientists to discover how and why materials change when they are heated or cooled, and how different families of substances react with each other to make new chemicals.

Doing the experiments

All the experiments in this book have been designed for you to do at home with everyday substances and equipment. They can also be done in your school laboratory. Always follow the safety advice given with each experiment. Ask an adult to help you when the instructions tell you to.

This pot changes color to show that the water has boiled—an example of a material change.

About Changes and Reactions

In science, the word *material* means any substance around us, from the wood in trees to the air we breathe. Materials are changing all the time. Just think about the changes that happen in nature throughout the year. During the winter, water can change into ice and snow. In spring, it changes back to water again. Leaves and twigs grow in the spring, then die, and fall from the trees and rot away in the autumn and winter. Solid rocks in Earth's crust can be changed into soft soil by the action of wind and rain. Now think about the kitchen and the food prepared in it. Ingredients in different foods, such as cakes and breads, change as they are cooked. Runny cake batter changes into solid cake. The substances change again when you eat and digest them. These are just a few examples of the ways in which materials change.

Material changes occur naturally in plants, animals, and Earth itself. We use them to our advantage at home and in many different industries, including the chemical industry. These changes sometimes make materials look different, feel different, or behave differently. They often even make entirely new materials that did not exist before.

*When you stir sugar into a drink, the crystals of sugar break apart. This is a **physical change.***

Why changes happen

Material changes don't just happen on their own—there is always a reason for them. In the examples given, water freezes or ice melts because the **temperature** goes down or up. Leaves and twigs rot away because they are eaten away by tiny **microorganisms** in the soil. Food in the oven changes because the temperature is very hot. It changes again when you eat it because it is broken up by your teeth and turned into simpler substances by chemicals in your digestive system.

*Firefighters try to put out a burning fire, which is an example of a **chemical change**.*

The atomic theory

Chemists think of substances as being made up of tiny **particles** that are too small to see. This is called the atomic theory. These particles are either individual **atoms** or atoms joined together by chemical **bonds** into groups called **molecules.** For example, in a metal, the particles are individual atoms. In water, the particles are molecules, each made up of two hydrogen atoms and one oxygen atom. The atomic theory helps us to understand how substances behave.

Physical and Chemical Changes

All material changes are either **physical** or **chemical changes.** In a physical change, only the physical **properties** change—the chemical properties stay the same. In a chemical change, the chemical properties change and new materials form. The physical properties of the new materials may be different from the original materials. Chemical changes are also called chemical reactions.

Imagine a piece of wood. If you cut the wood to make sawdust, the wood goes through a physical change. It becomes a powder instead of a strong material. While its physical properties have changed, it is still wood. But if you heat the wood, it burns and only gas and ashes are left. The wood is no longer wood, so it has gone through a chemical change.

Reversible and permanent changes

Chemical changes are usually permanent, while physical changes are not. In a permanent change, the changes made to a material cannot be reversed. Burning wood is an example of a permanent change, because ash cannot be turned back into wood. In a nonpermanent change, the change can be reversed. For example, water becomes ice when you put it in the freezer and turns back into water again when you thaw it.

A cake goes through a permanent change in the oven. The cake mixture can never be gotten back.

Experiment: Evidence of reactions

PROBLEM: How can we tell that a chemical change is happening?

HYPOTHESIS: We can look for signs of a chemical change, such as a change of color, escaping gas, or heat.

EQUIPMENT
balloon
small plastic bottle
funnel
vinegar
baking powder

Experiment steps

1. Push the funnel into the neck of the balloon. Pour a tablespoon of baking powder through the funnel into the balloon.

2. Pour about four teaspoons of vinegar into the bottle. Stretch the neck of the balloon over the neck of the bottle, making sure no powder falls out.

3. Lift up the balloon to make the powder fall into the bottle.

RESULTS: What happens to the balloon? What do you think is causing this? Is a chemical reaction taking place? You can check your results on page 47.

Changes of State

Solids, liquids, and gases are called states of matter. A change of state occurs when a substance changes from one state to another. For example, when ice (the solid form of water) changes to liquid water, the ice is said to have changed state. Changes of state usually occur when the **temperature** of a substance changes. As the temperature increases, substances change from solid to liquid and from liquid to gas. As the temperature decreases, they change from gas to liquid and from liquid to solid. There is a fourth state of matter, called plasma, but it does not occur naturally very often.

All changes of state are **physical changes.** So when a substance changes from one state to another, its physical **properties** change, but its chemical properties stay the same. Changes of state are also reversible changes. This means that when a substance changes state it can change back again. For example, if a piece of metal is heated until it changes state into a liquid, the change will reverse if the liquid metal is cooled.

This triangle shows the changes of state from solid to liquid to gas and back again.

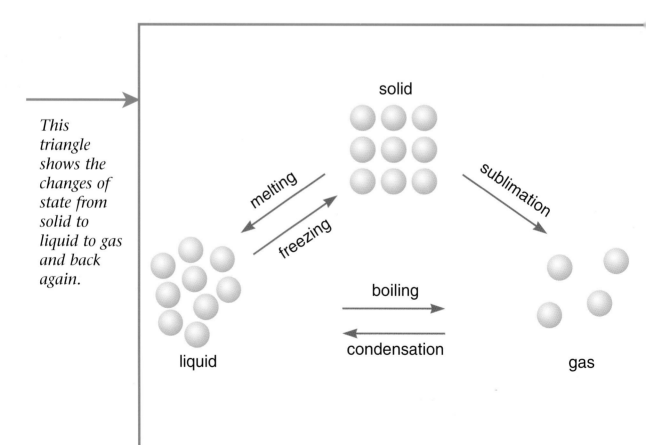

solid

melting

freezing

sublimation

boiling

condensation

liquid

gas

Melting and freezing

Melting is the change of state from solid to liquid. A particular substance always melts at a particular temperature, called the **melting point.** For example, the melting point of ice is 0°C (32°F). The melting point of iron is 1,535°C (2,795°F). Freezing is the change of state from liquid to solid. It is the opposite of melting and occurs as a substance cools. For any substance, its freezing point is the same temperature as its melting point.

Boiling and condensation

Boiling is the change of state from liquid to gas. A particular substance will always boil at a particular temperature, called the **boiling point.** The boiling point of water is 100°C (212°F). The boiling point of iron is 2,861°C (5,182°F).

Condensation is the change of state from gas to liquid. When a gas is cooled until its temperature reaches its boiling point, it **condenses** into a liquid.

Evaporation

Evaporation is a change of state from liquid to gas that takes place when the liquid's temperature is still below its boiling point. The **particles** in a liquid are constantly moving. Sometimes, particles moving upward at the surface escape into the air and become a gas. Puddles dry up because of evaporation. The water in them slowly escapes to become water **vapor** in the air. The water in the air condenses again if it hits a cold surface.

Some materials, such as solid carbon dioxide, change straight from solid to gas. This change is called sublimation.

Melting and Boiling Points

Changes of state occur when the **particles** in solids, liquids, and gases either break away from each other or join together. The particles themselves do not change in any way, which is why changes of state are not **chemical changes.**

When any substance is heated, its particles vibrate more and more. But the particles stay where they are because the **bonds** between them stay intact. When the **temperature** reaches the substance's **melting point,** the bonds between the particles begin to break. The particles are now free to move around, so the substance is now in its liquid state. If the liquid cools to below the substance's melting point, the bonds reform and the substance becomes a solid again.

When a substance in its liquid state is heated, its particles move faster and faster. When the temperature reaches the substance's **boiling point,** the particles break free from each other completely. The liquid has boiled to become a gas. If the gas cools below the substance's boiling point, its particles group together again, the bonds reform, and the substance **condenses** to become a liquid again.

White-hot liquid titanium—melting point 1,675°C (3,047°F)—is being poured into a mold to make ingots.

Different substances have different melting and boiling points. For example, water boils at 100°C (212°F), oxygen at -183°C (-297°F), and iron at 2,861°C (5,182°F). A material's melting and boiling points depend on how strong the bonds are between its particles. Materials with weakly joined particles have low melting and boiling points. Materials with strongly joined particles have high melting and boiling points.

More physical changes

Solids, liquids, and gases change in size or shape as they are stretched or **compressed.** Solids get slightly longer when you stretch them, because the bonds between the particles are stretched. They can't be easily compressed, because the particles are closely packed. The **volume** of a liquid decreases slightly when it is compressed, as the particles are forced closer together. Gases can be compressed much more than solids or liquids, because their particles are widely spread.

Solids, liquids, and gases also change in volume when they are heated or cooled. Solids expand when they are heated, because their particles vibrate more and so take up more space. Liquids expand when they are heated, because their particles move faster and collide more often and so take up more space. Gases expand when they are heated, because their particles move faster.

Ice is one of the few solids that are less dense than their liquid forms. This is why it floats.

Chemical Reactions

A chemical reaction happens when two or more substances react with each other. After the reaction, one or more new substances have been formed and the original substances have been altered. This means that during a chemical reaction, a **chemical change** takes place. The original substances are called the **reactants,** because they react together. The new materials are called **products.**

An example reaction

An example of a common chemical reaction is when gas on a stove burns. The reactants are the gas methane, which comes through the pipes, and oxygen, which is one of the gases in the air. During the reaction, two new substances—the products—are formed. They are carbon dioxide, which is a gas, and water **vapor,** which is water in gas form. The **particles** of oxygen, methane, carbon dioxide, and water vapor are **molecules.** During the reaction, the molecules of oxygen and methane break up and the **atoms** rearrange themselves to form molecules of carbon dioxide and water vapor. The reaction also produces a lot of heat energy, which is why we use gas for cooking!

Another reaction

When strips of magnesium are added to hydrochloric **acid,** the magnesium fizzes strongly because the acid reacts with it. This fizzing is made by bubbles of gas forming on the metal. The gas is hydrogen, which is one of the products of the reaction. Another product, called magnesium chloride, is also formed.

Nothing lost, nothing gained

Although reactants are altered and new products are formed during a chemical reaction, no atoms are lost or gained. All the atoms that are in the reactants are in the products. This means that the total **mass** of the reactants is the same as the total mass of all the products.

Magnesium reacts with hydrochloric acid.

Experiment: Changing substances

PROBLEM: How can we show that reactants change to products in a chemical reaction?

HYPOTHESIS: Burning is a reaction. When a substance burns, the products are gases. If these gases are allowed to escape, then the ash left will weigh less than the object that burned.

> **EQUIPMENT**
> matches and matchbox
> 6-in. (15-cm) ruler
> round pencil
> scissors
> tape

Experiment steps

1. Lay the pencil on a table top and stick it down with tape.

2 Attach a match to the end of the ruler with tape so the end for lighting hangs over.

3. Balance the ruler on the pencil. Be patient!

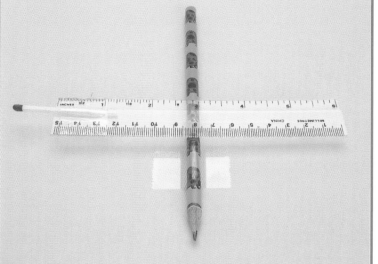

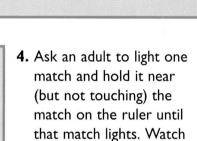

4. Ask an adult to light one match and hold it near (but not touching) the match on the ruler until that match lights. Watch what happens.

RESULTS: What happens to the ruler as the match burns? What does this tell you about the products of the chemical reaction? You can check your results on page 47.

Chemical Equations

A chemical equation is a way of writing down the changes that occur in a chemical reaction. It shows the **reactants** that take part in a reaction and the **products** that are made during the reaction. The reactants are written on the left side of the equation and the products on the right side. An arrow shows the direction in which the reaction happens, usually pointing from left to right.

Sometimes you will see a double arrow pointing in both directions. This means that the reaction is a reversible reaction and the products can react with each other to form the original reactants again.

Word equations

In a word equation, the reactants and products are shown by their chemical names. For example, below is the word equation for the reaction between carbon and oxygen. Carbon and oxygen are the reactants and carbon dioxide is the product.

carbon + oxygen	$\longrightarrow$	carbon dioxide
reactants	direction of reaction	product

Symbol equations

A **symbol** equation is an equation in which the reactants and products are represented by their chemical symbols and **formulas.** This is the symbol equation for the reaction above:

$C + O_2$	$\longrightarrow$	CO_2
reactants	direction of reaction	product

Balanced equations

In a symbol equation, the symbol for each **element** represents an **atom** of the element. Atoms cannot be lost or gained during a reaction, so there must be the same number of atoms of each element on each side of the equation. This is known as a balanced equation.

For example, magnesium and oxygen react to form magnesium oxide. In magnesium oxide, which is a solid, one atom of magnesium always combines with one atom of oxygen. Oxygen gas is made up of **molecules,** each of which contains two oxygen atoms. So two atoms of magnesium are needed to react with each oxygen molecule. This is the balanced symbol equation for the reaction:

magnesium + oxygen $\longrightarrow$ magnesium oxide
    2Mg   + O_2 $\longrightarrow$ 2MgO

The equation is balanced because there are two magnesium atoms and two oxygen atoms on each side of the equation.

When magnesium ribbon burns, the magnesium combines with oxygen.

Sodium reacts violently with water. The products are hydrogen gas and sodium hydroxide.

Here's the balanced equation for the reaction of sodium and water:

sodium + water $\longrightarrow$ hydrogen + sodium hydroxide
   2Na + $2H_2O$ $\longrightarrow$ H_2 +   2NaOH

Important Reactions

Thousands of different chemicals can react with each other, so there are millions of possible chemical reactions. Many reactions are similar to each other, even though the **reactants** and **products** may be different. For example, an **acid** will always react with a metal in the same way. So hydrochloric acid reacts with magnesium in the same way that sulfuric acid reacts with zinc. These similarities mean that we can classify chemical reactions into groups that are named after what happens to the reactants during the reaction. The following are groups of reactions that we often see in the laboratory and are often used in the chemical industry.

Synthesis

A synthesis reaction is a simple reaction in which two **elements** react together to form a **compound.** For example, if iron filings (which are made up of the element iron) and sulfur are heated together, they react to form iron sulfide:

$$\text{iron} + \text{sulfur} \longrightarrow \text{iron sulfide}$$
$$\text{Fe} + \text{S} \longrightarrow \text{FeS}$$

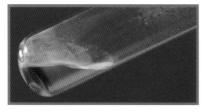

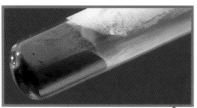

Mercury oxide decomposes on heating.

Decomposition

A decomposition reaction is a reaction in which a compound splits to make two or more different elements, or more simple compounds. Decomposition often happens when a material is heated, in which case it is called thermal decomposition. For example, mercury oxide, which is a red powder, decomposes when it is heated. The reaction makes liquid mercury metal and oxygen gas:

$$\text{mercury oxide} \longrightarrow \text{mercury} + \text{oxygen}$$
$$2\text{HgO} \longrightarrow 2\text{Hg} + \text{O}_2$$

Neutralization

A neutralization reaction is a reaction of a substance with either an acid or an **alkali,** which turns the acid or alkali into a **neutral solution.** An **acidic** or **alkaline** solution that becomes neutral is said to be neutralized. For example, if sodium hydroxide is gradually added to hydrochloric acid, the acid is neutralized. So is the sodium hydroxide. The products of the reaction are a salt and water:

hydrochloric acid + sodium hydroxide $\longrightarrow$ sodium chloride + water

$HCl \quad + \quad NaOH \quad \longrightarrow \quad NaCl \quad + H_2O$

Most neutralization reactions are used to neutralize acids. Any substance that neutralizes an acid is called a **base.** Magnesium hydroxide is a base. It is used in medicine for indigestion, because it neutralizes excess hydrochloric acid in the stomach.

Polymerization

A polymerization reaction is a reaction in which many small, simple **molecules** join together to make a much bigger molecule called a **polymer.** All plastics are polymers.

All these strong, flexible items have been manufactured from various polymers such as polyethylene.

Displacement

Sometimes one **element** in a **compound** is replaced by another during a reaction. The first element pushes out, or displaces, the second. This is called a displacement reaction. The most common example of a displacement reaction is when one metal displaces another metal from a compound. For example, if iron filings are added to a **solution** of copper sulfate, the iron displaces the copper. Iron sulfate (a solid) is formed, along with copper metal:

$$\text{iron} + \text{copper sulfate} \longrightarrow \text{iron sulfate} + \text{copper}$$
$$\text{Fe} + \text{CuSO}_4 \longrightarrow \text{FeSO}_4 + \text{Cu}$$

One metal displaces another metal in a displacement reaction, because the first metal is more reactive than the other metal. This means that it is easier for the first metal to form compounds with other elements than it is for the second metal.

By writing down which metals displace which other metals in displacement reactions, you can compile a list of metals in order of how reactive they are. The most reactive metals are at the top and the least reactive at the bottom. This list is called a reactivity series. A metal will be displaced in a reaction by any metal above it in the series.

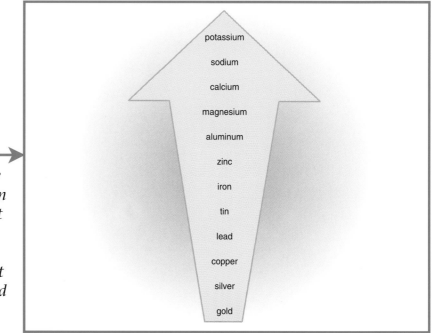

In this reactivity series of common metals, the most reactive metals are listed at the top and the least reactive are listed at the bottom.

potassium
sodium
calcium
magnesium
aluminum
zinc
iron
tin
lead
copper
silver
gold

A displacement reaction

How does a displacement reaction happen?

If you made a solution of a salt that contains one metal, and you dropped into it a piece of a metal higher on the reactivity series, the first metal should be displaced by the second, more reactive metal.

1. This test tube contains copper sulfate solution. A piece of magnesium ribbon is then dropped into the test tube.

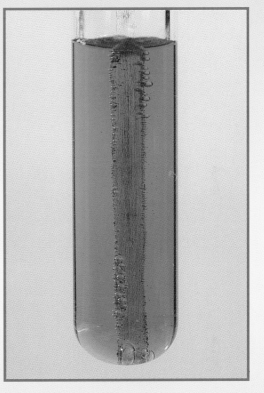

2. The magnesium is more reactive than the copper, so it displaces the copper from the solution. Colorless magnesium sulfate forms, which stays dissolved in the solution. Brown copper metal forms on the magnesium.

magnesium	+	copper sulfate	$\longrightarrow$	copper	+	magnesium sulfate
Mg	+	$CuSO_4$	$\longrightarrow$	Cu	+	$MgSO_4$

Oxidation and Reduction

An oxidation reaction is any reaction in which oxygen is added to a substance. The **product** of the reaction is normally a substance called an oxide. An oxide is a **compound** made up of an **element** combined with oxygen, such as carbon monoxide or copper oxide. The most common form of oxidation occurs when an element combines with oxygen in the air. During oxidation, the substance that combines with oxygen is said to be oxidized. In the reaction below, the magnesium is oxidized because it gains oxygen:

$$\text{magnesium} + \text{oxygen} \longrightarrow \text{magnesium oxide}$$
$$2Mg + O_2 \longrightarrow 2MgO$$

Reduction

Reduction is the opposite of oxidation. A reduction reaction is any reaction in which oxygen is removed from a substance. During reduction, the substance that loses oxygen is said to be reduced. The thermal decomposition of mercury oxide is an example of a reduction reaction. The mercury in the oxide is reduced because it loses oxygen:

$$\text{mercury oxide} \longrightarrow \text{mercury} + \text{oxygen}$$
$$2HgO \longrightarrow 2Hg + O_2$$

Redox

Redox stands for **red**uction/**ox**idation. So a redox reaction is a reaction in which both reduction and oxidation take place. Reduction and oxidation always happen at the same time. You cannot have one without the other. During a redox reaction, oxygen is removed from one substance and added to another. A redox reaction takes place when hydrogen gas flows over lead oxide. The products of the reaction are lead and water:

$$\text{lead oxide} + \text{hydrogen} \longrightarrow \text{lead} + \text{water}$$
$$PbO + H_2 \longrightarrow Pb + H_2O$$

Because lead metal is formed, oxygen must have been removed from the lead oxide. So the lead oxide has been reduced. At the same time, oxygen has been added to the hydrogen, forming water. So the hydrogen has been oxidized.

Redox in industry

The reaction that takes place inside a blast furnace—where iron is obtained from iron **ore**—is an example of redox at work in industry. Inside the hot furnace, carbon monoxide reacts with the iron ore (which is iron oxide). The iron oxide is reduced, leaving **molten** iron. The carbon monoxide is oxidized, creating carbon dioxide.

$$\text{carbon monoxide} + \text{iron oxide} \longrightarrow \text{iron} + \text{carbon dioxide}$$

$$3CO + Fe_2O_3 \longrightarrow 2Fe + 3CO_2$$

Electrolysis

Electrolysis involves using energy to split a **compound.** It works with any substance made up of charged **particles** called **ions.** Negative ions have more **electrons** than **protons.** Positive ions have more protons than electrons. When a substance is in **solution,** or melted, the ions can move.

A circuit is made with a power source and two **electrodes** dipped into the substance. One electrode is positive and one is negative. When a current passes through the substance, the negative ions are attracted to the positive electrode and the positive ions are attracted to the negative electrode. At the electrode, the ions lose or gain electrons to become **atoms** with no charge once more.

Using electrolysis

Electrolysis has several industrial applications, including metal extraction and electroplating.

Aluminum is extracted from its **ore,** aluminum oxide, by electrolysis. The aluminum ions in the **molten** ore move to an electrode, where aluminum metal forms and can be collected. Sodium is extracted from molten sodium chloride in the same way.

Electroplating involves coating a metal object with a layer of another metal. The metal object is used as an electrode during electrolysis. The ions it attracts form the coating. Tin cans are made from steel with a coating of tin created by electroplating.

Experiment: Electrolysis of water

PROBLEM: How can we separate water into oxygen and hydrogen?

HYPOTHESIS: We can try using electrolysis, since some water **molecules** break up into ions.

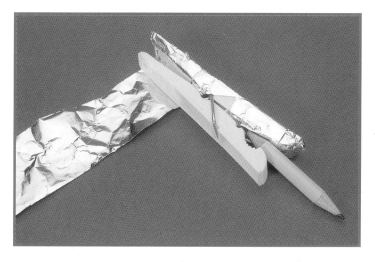

EQUIPMENT
double-pointed pencil
clothes pin
aluminum foil
AA battery
jar or glass

Experiment steps

1. Pour water into the jar until it is 3/4 in. (2 cm) below the rim.

2. Wrap some aluminum foil around one of the jaws of the clothespin. Clamp the clothespin onto the rim of the jar so that the jaw with the foil is on the inside. Use the clothespin to clamp the pencil onto the inside of the jar. The clothespin should be above the water and the pencil lead should be in it. Make sure the top end of the pencil lead is in contact with the aluminum foil.

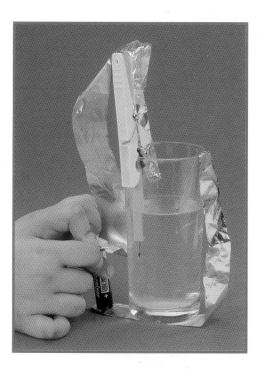

3. Cut a strip of aluminum foil about 8 in. (20 cm) long and 3/4 in. (2 cm) wide. Wrap one end of this around the foil on the jaw, but leave about 6 in. (15 cm) free at the other end.

4. Cut a strip of aluminum foil about 12 in. (30 cm) long and 3/4 in. (2 cm) wide. Push one end of the foil into the water on side of the jar opposite the clothespin. Bend the foil over the rim of the jar and fold it underneath.

5. Connect the (+) terminal of the battery to the alumiium foil running from the clothespin, and connect the (−) terminal of the battery to the other piece of alumium foil. Watch what happens.

RESULTS: What do you see happening on the pencil lead and the foil? What do you think is causing this? You can check your results on page 47.

Common Reactions

Here you can find out about reactions that happen every day around—and sometimes inside—us! Some are vital for the life of plants and animals. Most are reactions that involve materials and oxygen in the air around us. They include combustion, fermentation, photosynthesis, respiration, and corrosion.

Combustion

Combustion, or burning, is the reaction of a substance with oxygen in the air. A combustion reaction always gives out energy. It is an example of an exothermic reaction. *Exothermic* means "gives out heat."

Combustion does not usually start on its own. For example, you need to heat the wick of a candle with a match to light it. The heat provides the energy to start the reaction. After that, the heat from the combustion reaction keeps the reaction going. Lighting the candle is similar to pushing a ball to get it rolling down a hill. Once it gets going, it keeps going.

Because combustion gives off heat and light, it is a useful reaction. We burn fuels such as oil, gas, coal, and wood to provide us with heat and light. A good fuel is one that gives off plenty of energy as it burns. **Fossil fuels,** such as methane (called "natural gas"), contain carbon and oxygen and produce carbon dioxide and water when they burn. Combustion is an oxidation reaction because oxygen is added to the substance.

$$\text{methane} \ + \ \text{oxygen} \ \longrightarrow \ \text{carbon dioxide} \ + \ \text{water}$$
$$CH_4 \ + \ 2O_2 \ \longrightarrow \ CO_2 \ + \ 2H_2O$$

*On a cold day you can see gases made by combustion, because water **vapor condenses** in the cold air.*

Antoine Lavoisier (1743–1794)

Frenchman Antoine Lavoisier was the first scientist to figure out that oxygen from the air combines with a substance when the substance burns. Lavoisier carefully measured the **mass** of a substance and the mass of the **products** after it burned. He found that the mass increased during the reaction. He concluded that a substance must have been added during the reaction, and this substance was oxygen. Lavoisier was also a lawyer and politician. He was executed during the French Revolution because of his wealth.

Fermentation

Fermentation is the reaction in which a sugar, such as glucose, is turned into alcohol and carbon dioxide. Fermentation does not occur on its own. It only occurs in the presence of a **microorganism** called yeast. Here is the equation for fermentation:

$$\text{glucose} \longrightarrow \text{ethanol} + \text{carbon dioxide}$$
$$C_6H_{12}O_6 \longrightarrow 2CH_3CH_2OH + 2CO_2$$

We use fermentation in baking and brewing. In baking, the carbon dioxide released forms bubbles in bread dough. This causes the bread to rise. In brewing, carbon dioxide makes alcohol. It also causes the formation of the bubbles and foam in beer.

More Common Reactions

Corrosion is the reaction of a metal with oxygen in the air. It often involves water as well. Corrosion causes the metal to turn into a metal oxide, which is much weaker than the metal. The more reactive a metal is, the faster it corrodes. Metals at the top of the reactivity series, such as sodium, corrode instantly in the air. Metals at the bottom of the series, such as gold, don't corrode at all, which is why they are used for jewelery.

The most common form of corrosion is rusting, which is the corrosion of iron and steel. The flaky, red-brown rust is called iron oxide. Here is an equation for the reaction:

$$\text{iron} + \text{oxygen} \longrightarrow \text{iron oxide}$$
$$4Fe + 3O_2 \longrightarrow 2Fe_2O_3$$

Corrosion of sodium

Sodium is high on the reactivity series, so it corrodes very quickly.

1. A piece of sodium is removed from the oil it is stored in. The oil keeps air and water away from the sodium.

2. The sodium it cut to reveal a fresh metal surface. The surface is observed.

3. The surface very quickly changes color as the sodium reacts with the air to form sodium oxide. Sodium corrodes very quickly.

Photosynthesis

Photosynthesis is the reaction that takes place in the leaves of plants. Carbon dioxide from the atmosphere and water from the ground react together to make a carbohydrate. The carbohydrate is the food the plant needs to grow and live.

Photosynthesis needs energy to work. The reaction actually takes in energy, unlike combustion, which gives out energy. It is an example of an endothermic reaction. *Endothermic* means "takes in heat." The energy needed for photosynthesis comes from sunlight as it hits the leaves.

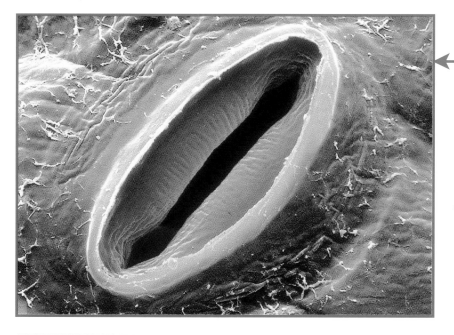

A photomicrograph of the underside of a leaf shows holes called stomata where carbon dioxide enters for photosynthesis.

carbon dioxide	+	water	$\longrightarrow$	sugar	+	oxygen
$6CO_2$	+	$6H_2O$	$\longrightarrow$	$C_6H_{12}O_6$	+	$6O_2$

Respiration

Respiration is the opposite of photosynthesis. Sugar and oxygen are turned to carbon dioxide and water. The reaction is exothermic. It releases energy that animals and plants use to make new chemicals. In animals, the energy is also used for movement.

sugar	+	oxygen	$\longrightarrow$	carbon dioxide	+	water
$C_6H_{12}O_6$	+	$6O_2$	$\longrightarrow$	$6CO_2$	+	$6H_2O$

Speeds of Reactions

The speed at which a reaction happens is called the rate of reaction. Some reactions naturally happen quickly, while others naturally happen slowly. For example, sodium and dilute hydrochloric **acid** fizz violently because they react very quickly, but iron and dilute hydrochloric acid react together much more slowly. However, the rate of any reaction can be increased in several ways.

More collisions are better

Reactions can only happen when the **particles** of the **reactants** touch each other. So the more chances that the particles have to collide with each other, the faster a reaction will happen. Liquids and gases react together more quickly than solids, because their particles can mix easily.

One way to increase the speed of a reaction in which one of the reactants is a solid is to cut the solid into small pieces. This increases the surface area of the solid so more collisions can occur. For example, the reaction between hydrochloric acid and iron filings is much faster than the reaction between the acid and a block of iron.

Another way of increasing the rate of a reaction is to increase the **temperature** of the reactants. Heat causes particles to move faster, so they collide more often and with more energy. Reactions also go faster if the concentration of a **solution** or the pressure of a gas is increased.

Dividing a piece of a solid into eight pieces doubles its surface area. This would double the rate of a reaction in which it took part.

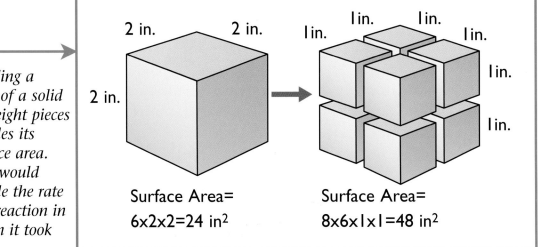

2 in.   2 in.

2 in.

Surface Area=
6x2x2=24 in^2

1 in.   1 in.
1 in.   1 in.
                1 in.
                1 in.

Surface Area=
8x6x1x1=48 in^2

Catalysts

A catalyst is a substance that increases the rate of a reaction. A catalyst takes part in a reaction, but at the end of the reaction it is the same as it was at the start. It does not change, it simply helps the process.

Chemical industries use catalysts to help make most of the chemicals they produce, such as plastics, acids, and fertilizers. Using a catalyst often means reactions can take place at room temperature, which saves energy that would otherwise be spent on heating the reactants. Catalysts also make the reactions more efficient, so that more chemicals can be produced. Rare metals often work as catalysts. For example, the catalytic converter in a car's exhaust system uses platinum and rhodium to turn harmful engine gases into harmless ones.

This powder is a catalyst used in oil refining.

Danger in the mines

Coal is mined from under the ground. It is a good fuel, but it has to be heated to a high temperature to start it burning, and then it burns quite slowly. On the other hand, coal dust, which is created in mines as the coal is dug out, burns so quickly that it can explode. This is because the dust has a huge surface area. Explosions of coal dust can be set off by tools making tiny sparks, or by lighting a match, and they have caused many mine disasters.

Changing the Speed of Reactions

Just as the rate of a reaction can be increased, it can also be decreased. We often slow the rate of reactions that we don't want to happen. There are also ways of stopping unwanted reactions, such as rusting and burning. For example, there are two ways of slowing down the reactions that make food rot. We reduce the **temperature** of the food by putting it in a refrigerator and we add **inhibitors** called additives to the food.

Preventing rusting

Rusting of steel is an expensive problem. The easiest way to stop rusting is to cover the steel to keep air and water from reaching it. This can be done with paint, plastic, grease, or another metal, such as zinc, that will corrode instead of the steel. Covering steel with zinc is called galvanization.

Fighting fires

A fire needs three things to keep it going: fuel, oxygen, and heat. One of these three things must be removed to stop the reaction. For example, fires can be put out by covering them with a blanket or with thick foam from a fire extinguisher, or by putting a burning object underwater. All of these remove the supply of oxygen. Heat can be removed by spraying cool water onto a fire. Water cannot be used on electrical fires because it conducts electricity. It cannot be used on oil fires because the oil floats on top of the water.

Galvanized iron trash cans do not rust even when some zinc is scratched off, because the zinc corrodes instead. Zinc corrodes much more slowly than steel.

Experiment: Putting out a candle

PROBLEM: How can we put out a fire?

HYPOTHESIS: One method of putting out a fire is to remove the oxygen that takes part in the combustion reaction.

EQUIPMENT
small candle
modeling clay
old saucer
glass jar

Experiment steps

1. Place a candle in the center of an old saucer. You might want to stick it down firmly with the modeling clay.

2. Stick a strip of clay around the rim of the jar.

3. Ask an adult to light the candle. Once it is burning evenly, turn the jar upside down over the candle. Press it down to seal the rim. Watch what happens.

RESULTS: Wait a few seconds. What happens to the candle? What do you think has caused this? You can check your results on page 47.

Solutions

A **solution** is made when a solid, liquid, or gas dissolves in another solid, liquid, or gas. For example, if you stir sugar into water, the sugar dissolves, making a sugar solution. The substance that dissolves to form a solution is called the **solute.** The substance it dissolves in is called the **solvent.**

When a solute dissolves it seems to disappear, but it is actually still there. Its **particles** mix in with the particles of the solvent. The solution is a mixture of the particles of solvent and particles of the solute. Dissolving is only a **physical change,** not a **chemical change,** because the solute and solvent do not change chemically.

Soluble or insoluble

Water is a very good solvent. Thousands of different substances, such as salt and sugar, dissolve in it. These substances are said to be soluble in water. There are also many substances, such as metals, that do not dissolve in water. They are said to be insoluble in water. Some substances that are insoluble in water, such as oil-based paints, are soluble in other solvents, such as turpentine.

Liquids that dissolve in each other are said to be miscible. For example, water and antifreeze (the chemical ethylene glycol) are miscible. When they are put together, their particles mix completely together.

Liquids that do not dissolve together are described as immiscible. The vinegar and oil that make up salad dressing are immiscible. When they are stirred together, the particles of each liquid stick together in small clumps. But when the stirring stops, the clumps soon separate again.

This spray contains solvents that dissolve the grease and paint on the path.

Experiment: Keeping track of solutes

PROBLEM: Does a solute disappear when it dissolves?

HYPOTHESIS: We can tell whether the solute disappears by finding the total weight of the solute and solvent before dissolving and seeing if the total weight changes when the solute is dissolved in the solvent.

Experiment steps

1. Tie a piece of string to the hook of the coat hanger. Use the string to hang the coat hanger from a door handle or other hook.

2. Tie a piece of string around the neck of each jar. Use the string to tie a jar to each end of the coat hanger. Make sure the jars hang freely.

3. Fill each jar halfway with water. Place a teaspoon into one of the jars. Then add water to each jar until the coat hanger just balances.

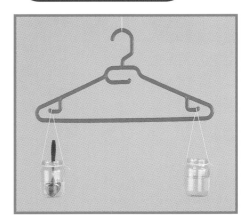

4. Cut a square of aluminum foil big enough to cover the top of a jar and fit it loosely over the jar with the spoon in it.

5. Put two teaspoons of salt on top of the aluminum foil. Carefully add some water to the other jar to balance the coat hanger again.

6. Lift the aluminum foil and pour the salt into the jar. Use the spoon in the jar to stir until the salt dissolves. Leave the spoon in the salt water and put the foil back on top of the jar. What do you notice?

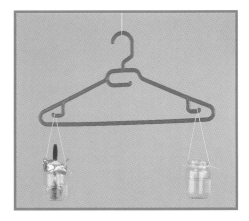

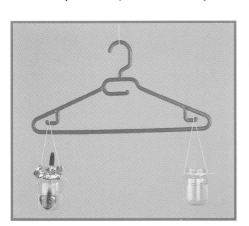

RESULTS: What happens to the coat hanger after the salt has dissolved in the water? What does this tell you about the solute in this solution? You can check your results on page 47.

Solubility

If you keep stirring salt into a glass of water, there comes a point where no more salt will dissolve. When the water cannot hold any more, we say that the **solution** is a saturated solution. The amount of a **solute** that will dissolve in a particular **solvent** before the solution becomes saturated is called its solubility. Solubility is measured in grams of solute per 100 milliliters of solvent. For example, the solubility of a salt in water might be 10 grams per 100 milliliters.

Changing solubility

The solubility of a solute normally changes with **temperature.** For example, the solubility of salt in water goes up as the temperature rises, which means that more salt will dissolve in hot water than cold water.

The solubility of most solids increases as the temperature increases. This means that the higher the temperature, the more solute needed to make a saturated solution. The solubility of gases normally decreases as the temperature rises.

A solubility curve is a graph that shows how the solubility of a particular solute in a particular solvent changes with temperature. The solubility is plotted up the vertical axis and the temperature is plotted along the horizontal axis.

As this saturated copper sulfate solution cools, it cannot hold as much dissolved copper sulfate, which forms crystals.

Experiment: Changing solubility

PROBLEM: Does sugar dissolve better in hot or cold water?

HYPOTHESIS: The solubility of solids increases with temperature, so more sugar should dissolve in hot water than in cold water. If a hot sugar solution is allowed to cool, some sugar will no longer be able to dissolve and crystals of sugar will form.

EQUIPMENT
clear measuring cup
sugar
spoon

Experiment steps

1. Ask an adult to heat a kettle of water. The water needs to be hot, but not boiling.

2. Pour about 1/2 cup (100 ml) of the hot water into the measuring cup.

3. Add some sugar and stir to dissolve it. Keep adding sugar until no more will dissolve. It will be very sticky! This is a saturated solution of sugar.

4. Let the sugar solution cool down and watch what happens.

RESULTS: As the solution cools down, what happens to the sugar? What does this tell you about the solubility of sugar at different temperatures? You can check your results on page 47.

The Rock Cycle

Over hundreds of millions of years, **physical** and **chemical changes** have happened to the rocks in Earth's crust to create the landscape we see today.

Types of rock

There are three types of rock in the earth's crust—igneous rocks, sedimentary rocks, and metamorphic rocks.

Igneous rocks are formed when **molten** rock called magma, formed deep beneath Earth's surface, cools and hardens. If it spews from a volcano as lava, the magma cools quickly and forms dark rock made of tiny crystals. If the magma cools slowly underground, it forms lighter rock with larger crystals.

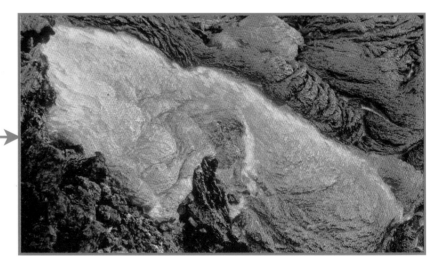

Thick lava has cooled quickly to form this igneous rock called pillow lava.

Sedimentary rocks are formed when tiny **particles** of rock settle on the bottoms of rivers, seas, and oceans, and form layers. Over time these layers become buried deep underground. The pressure of the layers above eventually squeezes out all the water, and the particles **compress** to make solid rock. Sedimentary rocks often contain the remains of animals and plants, which may be found as fossils. Limestone is a sedimentary rock made up almost completely from the shells of tiny sea creatures.

Metamorphic rocks are rocks that form when the chemical **properties** of igneous rocks and sedimentary rocks are changed by high **temperatures** or high pressure deep underground. For example, magma flowing into the cracks of a sedimentary rock can change the part of the rock next to the cracks into metamorphic rock.

Weathering

Weathering is the wearing away of rocks exposed at the earth's surface. Physical weathering breaks rocks into smaller pieces. The wind creates physical weathering by blowing particles of soil around, which wear away rocks. Water also creates physical weathering by washing loose rock away and carrying it along rivers, where it causes more weathering. Ice creates physical weathering by forming in cracks and splitting rocks apart. Rocks are also weakened as they expand and contract as the temperature changes.

Chemical weathering occurs when substances react with rocks and turn them into new substances. For example, **acid** rain reacts with limestone, forming substances that are washed away in the rain water. This slowly eats away the limestone, forming underground caves.

The rock cycle

The rock cycle is the slow circulation of rocks through Earth's crust over a period of hundreds of millions of years. For example, weathered rock is washed into the seas, where it forms new sedimentary rocks, while rocks deep underground melt to become magma, which can move back to the surface.

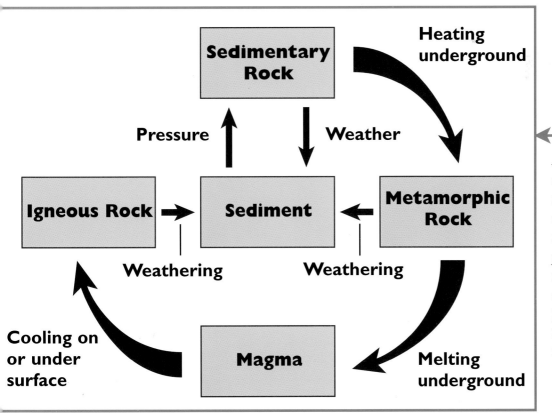

A diagram of an imaginary section of the earth's crust shows the processes involved in changing rocks from one type to another in the rock cycle.

The Periodic Table

The periodic table is a chart of all the known **elements.** The elements are arranged in order of their atomic numbers, but in rows, so that elements with similar **properties** are underneath each other. The periodic table gets its name from the fact that properties repeat themselves every few elements, or periodically. The position of an element in the periodic table gives an idea of what its properties are likely to be.

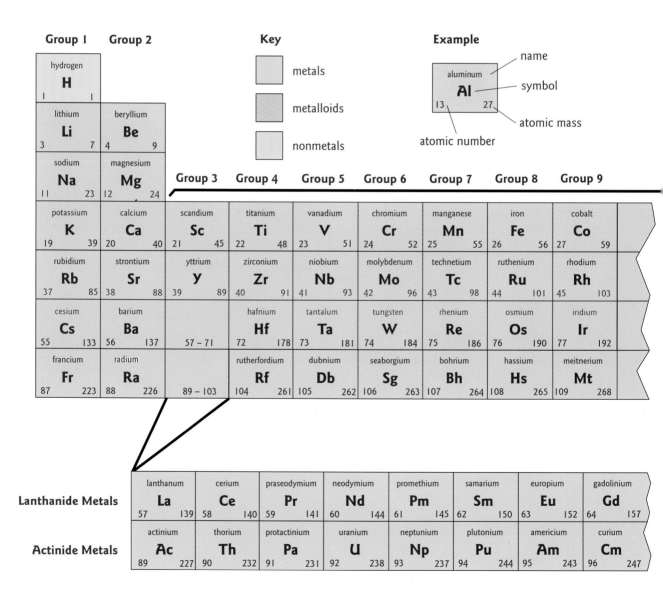

Key
- metals
- metalloids
- nonmetals

Example

name
aluminum
Al
symbol
13   27
atomic mass
atomic number

Group 1	Group 2	Group 3	Group 4	Group 5	Group 6	Group 7	Group 8	Group 9
hydrogen **H** 1 1								
lithium **Li** 3 7	beryllium **Be** 4 9							
sodium **Na** 11 23	magnesium **Mg** 12 24							
potassium **K** 19 39	calcium **Ca** 20 40	scandium **Sc** 21 45	titanium **Ti** 22 48	vanadium **V** 23 51	chromium **Cr** 24 52	manganese **Mn** 25 55	iron **Fe** 26 56	cobalt **Co** 27 59
rubidium **Rb** 37 85	strontium **Sr** 38 88	yttrium **Y** 39 89	zirconium **Zr** 40 91	niobium **Nb** 41 93	molybdenum **Mo** 42 96	technetium **Tc** 43 98	ruthenium **Ru** 44 101	rhodium **Rh** 45 103
cesium **Cs** 55 133	barium **Ba** 56 137	57 – 71	hafnium **Hf** 72 178	tantalum **Ta** 73 181	tungsten **W** 74 184	rhenium **Re** 75 186	osmium **Os** 76 190	iridium **Ir** 77 192
francium **Fr** 87 223	radium **Ra** 88 226	89 – 103	rutherfordium **Rf** 104 261	dubnium **Db** 105 262	seaborgium **Sg** 106 263	bohrium **Bh** 107 264	hassium **Hs** 108 265	meitnerium **Mt** 109 268

Lanthanide Metals

lanthanum **La** 57 139	cerium **Ce** 58 140	praseodymium **Pr** 59 141	neodymium **Nd** 60 144	promethium **Pm** 61 145	samarium **Sm** 62 150	europium **Eu** 63 152	gadolinium **Gd** 64 157

Actinide Metals

actinium **Ac** 89 227	thorium **Th** 90 232	protactinium **Pa** 91 231	uranium **U** 92 238	neptunium **Np** 93 237	plutonium **Pu** 94 244	americium **Am** 95 243	curium **Cm** 96 247

The vertical columns of elements are called groups. The horizontal rows of elements are called periods. Some groups have special names:

Group 1: **Alkali metals**
Group 2: **Alkaline** earth metals
Groups 3–12: Transition metals
Group 17: Halogens
Group 18: Noble gases

The table is divided into two main sections, the metals and **nonmetals.** Between the two are elements that have some properties of metals and some of nonmetals. They are called semimetals or metalloids.

			Group 13	Group 14	Group 15	Group 16	Group 17	Group 18
								helium **He** 2 4
			boron **B** 5 11	carbon **C** 6 12	nitrogen **N** 7 14	oxygen **O** 8 16	fluorine **F** 9 19	neon **Ne** 10 20
Group 10	Group 11	Group 12	aluminum **Al** 13 27	silicon **Si** 14 28	phosphorus **P** 15 31	sulfur **S** 16 32	chlorine **Cl** 17 35	argon **Ar** 18 40
nickel **Ni** 28 59	copper **Cu** 29 64	zinc **Zn** 30 65	gallium **Ga** 31 70	germanium **Ge** 32 73	arsenic **As** 33 75	selenium **Se** 34 79	bromine **Br** 35 80	krypton **Kr** 36 84
palladium **Pd** 46 106	silver **Ag** 47 108	cadmium **Cd** 48 112	indium **In** 49 115	tin **Sn** 50 119	antimony **Sb** 51 122	tellurium **Te** 52 128	iodine **I** 53 127	xenon **Xe** 54 131
platinum **Pt** 78 195	gold **Au** 79 197	mercury **Hg** 80 201	thallium **Tl** 81 204	lead **Pb** 82 207	bismuth **Bi** 83 209	polonium **Po** 84 209	astatine **At** 85 210	radon **Rn** 86 222
ununnilium **Uun** 110 281	unununium **Uuu** 111 272	ununbium **Uub** 112 285		ununquadium **Uuq** 114 289				

terbium **Tb** 65 159	dysprosium **Dy** 66 163	holmium **Ho** 67 165	erbium **Er** 68 167	thulium **Tm** 69 169	ytterbium **Yb** 70 173	lutetium **Lu** 71 175
berkelium **Bk** 97 247	californium **Cf** 98 251	einsteinium **Es** 99 252	fermium **Fm** 100 257	mendelevium **Md** 101 258	nobelium **No** 102 259	lawrencium **Lr** 103 262

The Reactivity Series

The reactivity series is a list of common **metals** in order of their reactivity. The most reactive metals are at the top and the least reactive at the bottom. This list gives the reactions of metals with air, water, and **acid.**

Metal	Symbol	Air	Water	Acid
potassium	K	Burns easily	Reacts with cold water	Violent reaction
sodium	Na	Burns easily	Reacts with cold water	Violent reaction
calcium	Ca	Burns easily	Reacts with cold water	Violent reaction
magnesium	Mg	Burns easily	Reacts with steam	Very reactive
aluminum	Al	Reacts slowly	Reacts with steam	Very reactive
zinc	Zn	Reacts slowly	Reacts with steam	Somewhat reactive
iron	Fe	Reacts slowly	Reacts with steam	Somewhat reactive
lead	Pb	Reacts slowly	Reacts slowly with steam	Reacts very slowly
copper	Cu	Reacts slowly	No reaction	No reaction
silver	Ag	No reaction	No reaction	No reaction
gold	Au	No reaction	No reaction	No reaction

Common Elements

Here is a table of the most common **elements** from the periodic table that you may come across at home or in a laboratory. The table indicates whether the element is a solid, liquid, or gas at room **temperature**. **Melting** and **boiling points** are for pure chemicals.

Element	Symbol	State at room temperature	Melting point (°C)	(°F)	Boiling point (°C)	(°F)
hydrogen	H	gas	-259	-434	-253	-423
helium	He	gas	-272	-458	-269	-452
lithium	Li	solid	180	356	1,342	2,448
carbon	C	solid	3,730	6,746	4,830	8,726
nitrogen	N	gas	-210	-346	-196	-321
oxygen	O	gas	-218	-360	-183	-297
fluorine	F	gas	-220	-364	-188	-306
neon	Ne	gas	-249	-416	-246	-411
sodium	Na	solid	98	208	883	1621
magnesium	Mg	solid	650	1,202	1,090	1,994
aluminum	Al	solid	660	1,220	2,519	4,566
silicon	Si	solid	1,414	2,577	2,900	5,252
phosphorus	P	solid	44	111	280	536
sulfur	S	solid	113	235	444	831
chlorine	Cl	gas	-101	-150	-34	-30
argon	Ar	gas	-189	-308	-186	-303
potassium	K	solid	63	145	759	1,398
calcium	Ca	solid	842	1548	1,487	2,709
iron	Fe	solid	1,535	2,795	2,861	5,182
copper	Cu	solid	1,083	1,981	2,595	4,703
zinc	Zn	solid	420	788	907	1,665
bromine	Br	liquid	-7	19	59	138
silver	Ag	solid	961	1,762	2,210	4,010
tin	Sn	solid	232	450	2,270	4,118
iodine	I	solid	114	237	184	363
gold	Au	solid	1,063	1,945	2,970	5,378
mercury	Hg	liquid	-39	-38	357	675
lead	Pb	solid	327	621	1,744	3,171

Glossary

acid liquid that is sour to taste, that can eat away metals, and is neutralized by alkalis and bases. Acids have a pH below 7.

acidic describes a liquid that has a pH below 7. All acids are acidic. Acidic also describes solids or gases that dissolve in water to make acids.

alkali liquid that feels soapy, that is corrosive, and is neutralized by acids. Alkalis have a pH above 7.

alkaline describes a liquid that has a pH above 7. All alkalis are alkaline. Alkaline also describes solids or gases that dissolve in water to make alkalis.

atom extremely tiny particle of matter. An atom is the smallest particle of an element that can exist. All substances are made up of atoms.

base any chemical that neutralizes an acid. Some bases dissolve in water to make alkalis.

boiling point temperature at which a substance changes state from liquid to gas

bond chemical connetion between two atoms, ions, or molecules

chemical change process in which two chemicals (called reactants) react together to form new chemicals (called products)

compound substance that contains two or more different elements joined together by chemical bonds

compress to squeeze into a smaller shape or space

condense to change from a gas into a liquid

electrode solid electrical conductor, usually graphite or metal, that is in contact with the liquid in electrolysis

electron extremely tiny particle that is part of an atom. Electrons are negatively charged and move around the nucleus of an atom.

element substance that contains just one type of atom. An element cannot be changed into simpler substances.

formula collection of symbols and numbers that represents an element or compound. It shows what elements are in a compound and the ratio of the numbers of atoms of each element.

fossil fuel fuel formed from the remains of ancient plants and animals. Coal, oil, and gas are fossil fuels.

inhibitor substance that slows the speed of a reaction. It is the opposite of a catalyst.

ion type of particle. An ion is an atom that has lost or gained one or more electrons, giving it an overall positive or negative charge.

mass amount of matter in an object, usually measured in grams or kilograms

melting point temperature at which a substance changes state from solid to liquid as it warms up

microorganism living thing too small to see without a microscope

molecule type of particle made up of two or more atoms joined together by chemical bonds. The atoms can be of the same element or different elements.

molten describes the liquid form of a substance that is normally a solid, such as a metal

neutral describes a substance that is neither an acid nor an alkali. It has a pH of 7. Water is a neutral liquid.

ore material dug from the ground that contains useful elements, such as iron, aluminum or sulfur

particle very tiny piece of a substance, such as a single atom, ion, or molecule

physical change process in which only the physical properties of a substance change. Changes of state are physical changes.

polymer compound that has molecules made up of many small molecules, all the same, joined together in a long chain

product chemical made during a chemical reaction

property characteristic of a chemical, such as color, texture, and density

proton one of the types of particles that make up the nucleus of an atom. Protons are positively charged.

reactant chemical that takes part in a chemical reaction

solute substance that dissolves in a solvent to make a solution

solution substance made when a solid, gas, or liquid dissolves in a liquid. The substance that dissolves is called the solute and the liquid it dissolves in is called the solvent.

solvent liquid that a substance dissolves in to make a solution

symbol letter or letters used to represent an element in chemical formulas and equations

temperature hotness or coldness of a substance

vapor gas form of a substance that exists below the substance's boiling point

volume space that something takes up

Experiment Results

page 9: As the powder falls into the vinegar, the balloon should inflate. This shows that a gas is being made. A chemical reaction must be taking place.

page 15: As the match burns, the ruler tips back again. This shows that the match is lighter after it burns than before it was lit. Gases from the reaction must have escaped into the air.

page 25: Gas bubbles form on the pencil lead and the foil. The gases must be hydrogen and oxygen, the two elements that make up water.

page 33: After a few seconds, the candle goes out. All the oxygen in the jar has been used up, and burning cannot continue without an oxygen supply.

page 35: The coat hanger balances again when the salt dissolves in the water. This shows that the total weight of water and salt stays the same, even when the salt has dissolved and cannot be seen anymore. The salt is still there, but it has broken up into molecules that are too small to see.

page 37: As the hot sugar solution cools down, the extra sugar comes out of the solution as crystals. This shows that at a lower temperature, the solubility of sugar is also lower. More sugar can be dissolved in hot water than in cold water.

Further Reading

Fullick, Ann. *Chemicals in Action.* Chicago: Heinemann Library, 1999.

Gardner, Robert. *Science Project Ideas about Kitchen Chemistry.* Berkeley Heights, N.J.: Enslow Publishers, Inc., 2002.

Moje, Steven W. *Cool Chemistry: Great Experiments with Simple Stuff.* Madison, Wisc.: Turtleback Books, 2001.

Oxlade, Chris. *Illustrated Dictionary of Chemistry.* Tulsa, Okla.: EDC Publishing, 2000.

Snedden, Robert. *Changing Materials.* Chicago: Heinemann Library, 2001.

Stwertka, Albert, and Eve Stwertka. *A Guide to the Elements.* New York: Oxford University Press, 1999.

Index